This book is dedicated to individuals who are facing impossible situations and are seeking some inspiration in order to make it through the storm.

# DOWN FOR THE COUNT

---

## Bouncing Back from

## Life's Blows

*Compiled by Felicia C. Lucas*

### Volume II

His Glory Creations Publishing, LLC
Wendell, North Carolina

Cover Photo: Pixabay.com

Scripture references are used with permission from Zondervan via Biblegateway.com

ISBN: 978-1-7327227-8-1

We hope you enjoy this book from His Glory Creations Publishing, LLC. Our goal is to provide high-quality, thought provoking books that connect to your real needs and challenges. For more information on other books and products, go to www.hisglorycreationspublishing.com

Printed in the United States of America

# ACKNOWLEDGEMENTS

## AUTHOR FELICIA LUCAS

Thank you, God, for the opportunity to share my story along with my amazing contributing authors. To my husband, friend and business partner Kelvin, thank you for your support! I love you!!! To my children, family and friends who have consistently supported me on my literary journey. I appreciate each of you! To my His Glory Creations Publishing LLC team, thank you for everything! You Rock!

# AUTHOR DR. PATRICE CAGLE

First, I acknowledge God who is the most important person in my life! I thank Him for choosing me to go through, for being right there with me and for strengthening me to get through what I've been through, especially when it looked hopeless. Thank you to my mom (Shirley), dad (Thomas), sister (Felicia), brother (Chris), and nieces/nephews who continue to support me in all my endeavors. To my dad, who was recently diagnosed with cancer, I'm proud of the way you've handled yourself during uncontrollable circumstances, that God has already allowed me to witness several miracles in your life, and that our relationship has grown closer than I could ever imagine. I love you and am proud to be your daughter! Lastly, thank you to my publisher, Felicia Lucas, for providing an opportunity for women to come together and connect with each other, as well as share our stories with the world.

## AUTHOR MARY HOOKS

I would like to thank Jesus Christ the Lord over my life. For choosing me to do greater works here on earth. My wonderful children: Nevaeh Gardner and Alex McDowell Jr. for sharing their mommy with the world as I do the Lord's work. My baby sister Renee Hooks-Wright for supporting me along this journey every step of the way.

## AUTHOR PAMELA HORNE

First, I give Glory, Honor, and Praise to my Lord and Savior Jesus Christ. Thanks to my former Pastor and Aunt, the late Dr. Mae V. Horne for her prayers, teaching, impartation and speaking over my life. To my parents Frank and Bessie Horne for raising me and believing in my abilities. To the late Al Wiggins, my favorite college professor who instilled in me confidence in my gift to write and went out on a limb to make sure I graduated. To all the people who pushed me to publish my writing, especially Minister Diane Pace who encouraged me to take part in this book. To all my family and friends who pushed me over the years and believed in me. To my Sissy, Daphne who has been my biggest support. Love to all my brothers, Frank, Thomas, Martin, and Will; my sisters Melanie and Leanne and my big sister, the late Felecia Harris. To my cousin, Joyce Horne Waller for repeatedly pushing me to write. Thanks to the Women of Triumph and CEO Anna Lyons for igniting the passion for using my gifts. Thanks to all those who supported me.

## AUTHOR JOCELIN T. HOOD MCELDERRY

First, I would like to thank GOD, for the strength to share a portion of my story. To the Best Daughter in the world, Nicollette, you know how I feel about you. To my parents, thank you so much for your support in my endeavors. A very special thank you to Henry DeLaine, III for all you have done over the years.

## AUTHOR DIANE PACE

I would like to express my gratitude to the many people who saw me through this book. Thank You, God. Thank you to my publisher, Felicia Lucas for enabling me to publish this chapter. Thanks to my mother Frances Turner for my Godly upbringing. Thanks to Cassandra Lyon and Teresia Burroughs for believing in me. Thanks, Carolynn Robinson for encouraging me. I'm grateful to my daughter Renee Walker who prayed and encouraged me every step of the way. I'm grateful to my husband, Raymond Pace for the love, the support, always believing in me and encouraging me to share my testimony.

## AUTHOR NANYAMKA PAYNE

Thank you for being a Husband, Father, Uncle, Friend, Son, Cousin, Hero, Entrepreneur, Giver, Legend, Hard Worker but Christian. An authentic, bold, matchless, limitless, effortless, unchanging, selfless, unselfish giver that taught me how to increase my faith by watching you work until the very end! I dedicate this chapter to you,

Leon "Shine" Gibbs
May 20th, 1955 – March 9th, 2019

## AUTHOR LOUVANTA WHITE

I'm truly thankful and grateful to be A blessing to those around me. First, I would like to thank God. Without his love, grace, and mercy. I wouldn't be the person I am today. I would like to thank the love of my life, my beautiful daughter, my family, those close to me, and my extended families. Mrs. Felicia Lucas, special thanks to you for always being a great Author Coach and allowing me to be a part of your vision. Last, but not least to each of the readers who will be reading the stories of each author of this vision. You are truly appreciated!

# Table of Contents

# INTRODUCTION

**By Felicia C. Lucas**

Have you ever watched a boxing match? There are two individuals in the boxing ring who desire to win each round. The first few rounds normally go smooth. Each of the boxers are getting in a few punches to their opponent. As each round gets higher and higher, they begin to move slower and depending upon their level of tolerance of pain; they continue to fight back or endure the punches from their opponent.

Have you ever gone through something in life which shook the very core of your existence? Have you ever lost something or someone who was very close to you? Have you experienced a treacherous situation and you had no clue if and when you would make it through? Have you felt the blows of life which can cause an individual to fall down and be in a very dark and lonely stage in life?

Just as a boxer experiences those blows that cause them to fall to their knees, we sometimes go through situations that seem impossible for us to rise above. Down for the Count occurs when one of the opponents are knocked down in the ring, and they are unable to rise within ten seconds. This boxer who has been knocked down will lose the fight if they cannot get up before the referee counts to ten. 10-9-8-7-6.... GET UP....5-4-3-2, as the crowd begins to cheer...1—then the bell sounds to end the round.

This book speaks to the individual who is down, in a low place in life and they struggle to get back on their feet again. Just like in a boxing match, you can be making your way back up and then you may not have the strength to rise again. Generally, when this happens, the boxer's coach and the crowd begin to cheer and shout to encourage the boxer to keep moving.

The co-authors in this book share their stories of how they experienced some adverse situations and how they ultimately bounced back from it. Our desire is as you read each of our stories, you are inspired and encouraged to hang on. We want you to know that out there in this world there is someone who has a similar experience and ultimately bounced back!

# CHAPTER 1

Thou wilt keep him in perfect peace, whose mind is stayed on thee: because he trusteth in thee

**Isaiah 26:3 (King James Version)**

**Have You Lost Your Mind?**
**By: Dr. Patrice Cagle**

It's one of the best movie quotes ever, "Have you lost your mind!" as heard by Hilly (Bryce Howard) after eating some of Minny's (Octavia Spencer) "special" pie, in The Help. What exactly is the "mind?" The mind is that part of a person that enables them to be aware of the world and their experiences, to think, and to feel. It refers to a group of cognitive processes that include functions like thinking, planning, attention, memory, reasoning, consciousness, will and imagination, judgement, and perception. Have you ever been in a conversation with someone who doesn't appear to be as engaged in the conversation as you are and says,

"I'm sorry, I have a lot on my mind?" While you may be able to comprehend what may be going on, you may not necessarily understand how it relates to the mind. Our mind is responsible for our thoughts, concepts, memories, emotions, precepts, and intentions. Spiritually, the mind is associated with the human soul and can be empowered by the Holy Spirit. In the New Testament, the mind is often portrayed as the center of a person's ethical nature.

So getting back to the quote in the movie, I hadn't lost my mind in that sense, but I had lost my memory. As I was nearing the end of my fourth year as a Doctoral candidate in Spring 2017, it became apparent that something was wrong, that went beyond the normal cognitive and memory problems that came along with my medical condition. I've been living with a chronic disease for nearly 10 years and had been experiencing difficulty with concentration, attention problems, short term loss of memory and confusion for at least a year. I tried to improve the symptoms with various natural supplements recommended by my doctor, not realizing that there was a deeper issue. I just thought I was forgetful. That is until I began to reverse letters and words and couldn't grasp anything I read, which hadn't been a problem in the past. I couldn't remember the experiments I had recently completed nor specific details about the dissertation project I had been working on for the past several years. I also couldn't remember much of anything I'd written in my own book (My Sustainer). These symptoms were downright frightening and interfered with my daily life!

My self-confidence began to dwindle. At times I felt awkward but didn't want to express my frustration. I was hesitant about others knowing that I was struggling with my memory. I knew I was too young, but the thought crossed my mind if I was experiencing symptoms of dementia. I was worried because I had planned to finish and defend my dissertation in about a month so I could graduate in May (2017). I was also conducting job and postdoc interviews and needed to be on point! I was repeating questions to others. I forgot where I put things, got frustrated when I couldn't recollect my train of thought or had to stop in the middle of a sentence because I couldn't recall the words I wanted to say. I learned big words in college, but that didn't matter because I wasn't able to remember simple words. I recall speaking with the chairperson of my department about a reserving a room for my defense. I became stuck in my tracks when I couldn't remember one single verb that would fit into the sentence, "I'm trying to _____ a location for my dissertation defense." My voice went silent. Thank goodness he knew what I was trying to say (SECURE or FIND), and we were able to finish the conversation! I know you're probably thinking, that was an easy sentence. Well, I most certainly agree when you can say it without really thinking about it. However, that was not my experience during this time; it was nothing short of a struggle.

On Friday, February 3, 2017, I had been reading and re-reading the same paragraph in an article, trying to comprehend it when someone whispered into my spirit to check the side effects of a medication I was being prescribed. I searched the internet and took a glance at the side effects. There it was right in front of me, "problems with memory or concentration." I couldn't believe it! You mean to tell me all this time it was the medication! I immediately messaged my doctor who also agreed that the medicine may be causing the problem (she was not the doctor prescribing the medication for my health condition). Her next statement to me was, "You have to stop taking the medication." I already had an appointment scheduled with her the following Monday to have some neurological tests done to find out what was really going on (or to determine if I was really losing my mind). Isn't it amazing how God will allow you to go through a struggle until you get almost to (what you feel is) the breaking point, and then step in and turn the situation around, reveal the problem/solution to you, or just simply change your mindset! God definitely showed up for me, when I wasn't expecting Him (2 Peter 3:10). He's just that merciful, gracious, kind, and faithful! Never would I have ever thought to associate my symptoms with the medication, and neither did the prescribing doctor.

Once I had been evaluated and received the test results, I was still anxious. The prescribing doctor told me that the chance of recovery from the memory loss was good, so that wasn't my concern. I was on a time crunch with my oral and written defense, and I knew how painful my medical condition was at times WITH the medication. I didn't want to imagine how I would function WITHOUT taking it. Though medication-induced cognitive impairment is often reversible, not knowing how much memory and cognitive function I would regain and how fast, was difficult. However, I had to keep on reading, writing, praying, fasting, and meditating like I did before I knew what the problem was and where it was coming from. I knew deep down inside that God didn't bring me that far in life, in school, in my relationship with Him, to bring revelation only for me to still fail. Therefore, despite the difficult process of recovery and physical suffering without the medicine, failure was NOT an option for me. It shouldn't be an option for you either! I didn't quit during any part of this journey, even though I could've and probably would have if I had listened to the enemy (Satan). Like David who was greatly distressed because men were talking of stoning him (1 Samuel 30:6), I found strength in and encouraged myself in the Lord.

I had to keep my mind on Him (Isaiah 26:3; Philippians 4:7) by continuing to spend time with Him and consistently praise and worship Him, while I took care of my responsibilities at home and church. I went to class (except when I was physically unable to), made presentations, took care of my experiments in the lab, and was available to help others. I faltered along the way but was reminded that God didn't give me a spirit of fear; but of power, of love, and a SOUND MIND (2 Timothy 1:7). I cried out to Him in my distress, knowing that He would hear me, and save/deliver me (Isaiah 41:10; John 14:27). Continuing to function like I was already healed was important to me, especially since I believed that He would work it all out in His timing (Romans 8:28). Though I had to read the scriptures repeatedly sometimes, I stood on His word because I knew His timing was always perfect. He's never too late but always on time (2 Peter 3:8). After all, He had already done so much for me and brought me through in the past; you could never convince me that this or anything else was too hard for my God (Jeremiah 32:27)! Yes, in my natural abilities, this was impossible, but I firmly believed that ALL things are possible through Him (Matthew 19:26; Luke 1:37). I also knew that if I had enough faith to speak it into the atmosphere, God had enough power to perform it. Slowly but surely, I began to see memory improvements. I went as long as I could without medication and unbearable pain until I eventually started a different one. Being cautious but not afraid of its similar side effects, I continued to trust God through the process, and He helped me meet my personal goal of submitting my written dissertation BEFORE the official deadline and defend my dissertation on schedule. God is a HEALER (even of my health condition), and I truly thank Him (in advance)!

You may be wondering why God delayed revealing the main reason for my memory loss, but I understood God's sovereignty (1 Chronicles 29:11-12; Isaiah 46:9-10; Philippians 2:13) and trusted Him. I also believe there was a greater purpose in going through the entire situation; to deepen (strengthen) my relationship with Him, for His glory, and so that you will realize that no matter how much your mind plays tricks on you (as it will) or you go through circumstances in life, God is still in control. When you surrender to His will and turn it over to Him, He will work it out for you.

# CHAPTER 2

Blessed is the one who perseveres under trial because, having stood the test, that person will receive the crown of life that the Lord has promised to those who love him.

**James 1: 12 (New International Version)**

**Are You Okay?**
**By: Mary Hooks**

Check on your strong friend. A simple "Are you okay?" is much needed. People often see you pushing and making it happen that they forget to ask that simple question.

Every day is a battle between wrong and right. On September 23rd, 2018 I was baptized for the second time and was serious about my yes to Christ. I made a promise to God that I would walk with him, and I meant that thing wholeheartedly. I knew God had a greater need for me and I was determined to live it out. I told God YES. Yes to your will, YES to your way (I want whatever he wants for me). I began to seek God day and night as the Bible tells us to do. As I did that God began to show me things, reveal to me who people really were, and took away my desire for anything that was not of him. Continuously seeking after God, things began to fall into place, and I was able to publish my first book in December 2018 and given many opportunities to speak at different events. Now you see me on flyers, my book is floating around, and I'm hosting events. I know it seems great, doesn't it? "Man her life has really changed" some may say. "Mary is doing her thing" others may say. The reality of it is the calling on my life is not glitter and glam. Behind the books, flyers, and pictures it's a spiritual battle. Outside of all that, I must remain at the feet of God. I must keep him first and continue to commune with him daily. There are nights when I'm up praying for the world and praying for people I don't even know. There are many nights when I'm up pacing the floor back and forth warring in the spirit. The weight that is on my life is not easy, but with God's help, he makes the load light. People praise and show love, and I get many congratulations, but I have to say thank you and focus forward because it is so much bigger than that. God has assigned me to bring his people out of darkness to be a game changer to let the world know that he is real.

I didn't ask for this God chose me. I understand that I'm the only Bible some people will ever read. With that being said, there are some things that I can no longer do, some places I can no longer go, some people I can no longer entertain, and some things I can no longer participate in. There is a little saying that says do what makes you happy. I totally disagree; doing what makes us happy could get us in a lot of trouble. We must do only what glorifies God. We are here on earth to live a life that is pleasing to Christ. We must be determined to not let him down. Nobody is perfect. There are times when I fall short of his glory, but I never beat myself up about it.

When this happens, I then repent and ask God to strengthen me in whatever area I lack strength in. God gives us grace and mercy he wants us to call on him for help. ABBA (father) he loves to lead and guide his children; such a loving God. No matter what we have done, he is always there with his arms out. Just like we do our own children here on earth. He promises to never leave us nor forsake us, and I'm a witness that his word is true, and his word will never come back void. The more I read God's word, the stronger I get. His promises are right there to keep us even when life gets rough, to let us know everything is going to be alight. As I sit here and write this book, I'm reminded how God said he knew me before I was ever formed in my mother's womb. He knows the plans for me plans of good and not of evil. I never thought I would be an author it was never a desire of mine, but God has shown me that he is the author of my life and this is what he needs me to do to reach his people. I now deal with rejection, jealousy, and envy from people that I love dearly due to the calling on my life. It hurts because people don't want to see you do well. They would rather see you down and out. I had to really deal with this thing and ask God why are many of my love ones clowning me like this?

I would never treat them differently because they are accomplishing things, but you know God showed me that because of the calling that's on my life the devil will use anybody to try to knock me off focus. I now must love people from a distance and let God use me fully. He also showed me that people want to see you do good just not better than them. But he says love them anyways. With this anointing comes great judgement and even greater work. I remain standing strong only because I am strong in the Lord. He keeps me and keeps my mind at peace. I cannot allow the wrong things into my mind not even for a second. The mind is so powerful what we feed it is what we get. I don't even have a television in my home anymore because I now understand the things we watch and listen to molds us. We start to get urges and ideas from the things we see and hear. Just think about it the music today is talking about drugs, money, sex, and killing, and that's exactly what is going on around the world the crime rate is at an all-time high, and it is only getting worse. Once you understand and begin to pay attention to the way you react to situations after you get done watching reality/drama TV shows, you will see how powerful the things we see and hear really are.

This new journey for me is serious, and I pray for the Lord to increase my discernment daily. People from my past are constantly sending me messages via social media and email. I must remember why God removed them from my life and not get caught up in old times/ feelings. God makes no mistakes so when he removes someone from your life it is for your good. A good friend of mine says "You know your future-ready when your past wants you back." Ain't that the truth? The enemy doesn't want any of us to make it to destiny and live the life God intended for us to live. When God wants to bless you, he sends a person, and when the enemy wants to destroy you, he sends a person. I am so thankful for the wisdom, knowledge, and understanding that God has given me thus far. I know I have so much more learning to do. So be sure to reach out to people especially people that you know God has a great calling on their life. We are so busy caring for others that we often forget ourselves. We are so focused on doing what God has called us to do, so please before you assume anything to ask the simple question "Are you Okay?"

# CHAPTER 3

And we know that in all things God works for the
good of those who love him, who have been
called according to his purpose.

**Romans 8:28 (New International Version)**

**They Called Me Sarah- The Painful Struggle to
Walk in Healing**
**By: Elder Pamela Horne**

Over the years, I had struggled with sickness in my
body. There were phantom pains that would rip
through my stomach, painfully heavy periods,
backaches and extreme fatigue. I just always felt sick.
I would see myself in a casket at an early age. In the
dream, there were no children and no one to mourn my
passing. At times, I was convinced that I would not
make it to my forties. When I gave my life to Christ, I

began to declare: "I shall not die, but live, and declare the works of the Lord"-***Psalm 118:17***.

Seventeen years ago, I began to walk in healing, and that's when the attacks on my body intensified. My doctor wanted me to have a hysterectomy, but I was walking by faith and believing God for children one day. Every time I turned around, I was reminded of how old Sarah was when she gave birth to Isaac and people began to call me Sarah.

In 2004, I had surgery to remove fibroid tumors. My doctor said the surgery was a success and she had run dye through my fallopian tubes to ensure there was no blockage. Finally, I thought, it's over. One of my church members Lisa (name change) was also in the hospital, on the same floor. She needed to go on dialysis. When I returned home, I became very sick and ached all over. I called the doctor, and they gave me medication for nausea. A week later, I received a disturbing letter from the hospital. It sounded like something had gone wrong with the surgery at first, but the ending was worded like a routine follow-up after surgery.

Two weeks later, I went to church, I saw Lisa, and she asked me if I had heard what they had done to us in the hospital. I asked her what she was talking about. "You haven't seen it on the news," she asked? I hadn't watched the news on a regular in years. I had no clue that Duke hospital had a mix-up with hydraulic fluid and surgical equipment. It was awful. My joints had gotten so bad that I could barely get out of bed. My doctor sent me to a Duke Rheumatologist, who put me on medication for Rheumatoid arthritis. Lisa had found an attorney in Raleigh, and I decided to consult them also. The lawsuit grew and right before they took it to court; they dismissed my case and Lisa's. Eventually, Lisa grew sicker and kept getting staph infections. A couple of years later, she passed away.

I stopped taking the medication when my doctor said he couldn't diagnose me with Rheumatoid arthritis. Whatever it was had seemingly gone into remission. The pain that was left was manageable with over the counter pain meds. I didn't like the idea of taking medications that were dangerous to my eyesight, and I decided not to continue taking it if I didn't have the condition. The tumors grew back, and I had another surgery in 2006, still refusing to have a hysterectomy and suffering the pain and mental anguish of trying to block the doctor's negativity and hold on to the promises of God.

Over the next six years, I dealt with heavy bleeding and cramping associated with the tumors, which continued to grow. In 2010, the doctors said I was anemic and in need of iron pills. The following year, I began to have shortness of breath and could hardly walk from the parking lot into the building for work. I got really sick and thought I had the flu or something. During that time, my cycle had started staying on for weeks. This time, it would not go off, so I started seeing a new doctor. Over the weekend, I grew worse. I couldn't eat or stand up without getting dizzy. I was hemorrhaging and cramping, my joints ached, and my neck and back hurt. I couldn't work or leave the house.

At one point, I passed out from the pain and remembered feeling like my spirit had left my body. God was trying to show me something. All I remember is maneuvering through darkness and twine and asking God why I was sick. I prayed and bound the enemy and the works of witchcraft. The next day, I was able to get up and heat up some chicken noodle soup that one of my friends had made for me. I forced myself to eat. It had been four days. My doctor decided to give me a blood transfusion. I didn't want anyone else's blood, and I cried to God about it. After God said he was going to give me a transfusion of the blood of Jesus, I went through with the procedure and was able to return to work. In the meantime, my doctor tried pills, shots, etc. to stop the bleeding. Nothing worked, and I soon had lost all the blood that had been transfused into my body. I expressed the desire to preserve fertility, so my doctor and I decided the best route was to have a Uterine Fibroid Embolization procedure and another transfusion. After the procedure, I returned to work. In 2012, I had a gastric sleeve operation. My weight was hindering me, and I thought that it would help the neck and back pain from a 2008 work-related injury. I had gained close to 100 lbs. since that incident.

Worker's Comp had released me back to work and declared there was nothing else they could do for me; I needed to lose weight. I accepted my fate and tried to deal with the pain as best as I could. When my neck would hurt, I would lay my head back. This would cause me to go to sleep. I went back to Worker's Comp, and the doctor said, "I don't know why that is, but I can see you've gained weight, you just need to stop eating." There it was again, the gnawing reminder that I was fat. My friend once said, "I had to get delivered from the word fat." I didn't quite understand what she meant, but it truly is a struggle to get past that word and any insinuation that you eat more than the next person. Seeing skinny people eat more than me, not gain any weight and no stigmatism attached to their eating. If I picked up a piece of cake, I had to hear, "You don't need that." Eating bread was not good; I used too much sugar, etc. etc. The surgery was successful at first, then I stopped losing and started gaining weight again, I still couldn't exercise, and by this point, I needed knee replacement surgery, and I had to use a C-Pap machine. It was a vicious cycle. I couldn't lose weight without exercise and couldn't exercise to lose weight.

I knew that losing weight would help me feel better, but I felt hopeless in terms of being able to do it with diet and exercise so again, I got medical help. Time and time again, diets failed, and my joints worsened. I was desperately trying to lose weight, walking in healing and believing God for a husband and a baby. It felt like a never-ending Hell. If I gave up believing, then I failed to have faith. If I just had faith and didn't lose weight, then my faith meant nothing- Faith Without Works is Dead.

The enemy constantly reminded me of my situation and constantly played in my mind about infertility. I would go to a service, and the speaker would give me a Word from the Lord.... They called me Sarah! One after the next, they called me Sarah! God favored me. He was going to send my husband; I would have children! I didn't want to hear how Sarah had a baby in her old age; it didn't make me feel better. Instead, it felt like God Himself was mocking me. 45 years old, 48 years old, 50 years old, then 51, and finally 52 – who wants a baby at this age? After all, I went through to preserve my fertility- I was too old to care. I manage the joint pain with prayer, meds and other methods. I'm walking in my healing.  Bishop Noel Jones said it best at the midyear conference on February 19, 2019, at Love Temple in Goldsboro, NC when he said faith does not override His will!  He prayed for God to heal his mother and he had faith that God would do it, but it was God's will to take her home.  I had faith in God to bless me with children, and I fought the good fight of faith over the matter, but was it God's will for me to have a child? Time will tell, but if He doesn't do it, I know that He is able. So don't call me Sarah, my name is Pam.

# CHAPTER 4

And we know that GOD causes everything to work together for the good of those who love GOD and are called according to HIS purpose for them.

**Romans 8:28 (New Living Translation)**

**Not What You Think!**
**By: Jocelin T. Hood McElderry**

Sometimes life will give you lemons, and you must figure out how to make lemonade. So, I'm going to share with you this great opportunity that I was given to make lemonade despite what was going on in my life. Everyone thinks that just because a person looks like they're not having issues, they assume that their life is going well. I was one of those people that made struggle look easy because I dare not allow anyone to know that I was down. Let's take a quick trip together.

I was born into a two-parent household and had a good life for the most part. But there were some simple things I needed that I did not receive which set the tone for the rest of my life. Some of the choices I made were directly related to those needs. Life can teach you some of those things, but it is not always kind.

Love is a word that means many things to many people. Unfortunately, there are many that never get to understand the full meaning of love. I grew up in a time of implied love meaning that if they provided for you, then you could assume that you were loved. No real warmth of love just the assumption that if they provided a roof over your head and clothes on your back, then they loved you. But how many of you know that some of us required just a little more to grow into the greatest we can.

Webster gives the meaning of love as a feeling of strong or constant affection for a person arising out of kinship or personal ties; it also says a warm attachment, enthusiasm, or devotion. Interesting isn't it that too often we do not get to know the definition that we need the most.

What tends to happen is that we journey into life looking for the love we need in all the wrong places. I grew up searching for the warm type of love from all the wrong sources. I ended up in crazy relationships with the wrong men that were of my own choosing since I was very unclear on the real meaning of love as it pertained to me. The blessing is I have finally matured enough and dealt with some of the skeletons to be able to talk to other women and help them avoid some of the traps that befell me.

I was pretty much an only child although I had an older sister that really did not care for me very much. Being the type of person that I was, I did everything I could to try to make her like and love me. As a young child, it was easier, but as I grew older, I became painfully aware that it was not going to happen in that manner. People will tolerate you in order to get what they desire from you and then drop you until the next time they need you.

The power of love is amazing, and it can change the full trajectory of a person's life. It is like a flower that grows in a pot, the more you water the flower, talk to it and nurture it the stronger it grows, but if you forget to give it water or pay attention to it, then it eventually withers and dies. Love works in the same way it must be nurtured and watered with time, effort and energy in order to thrive and survive. Children need the warm love, disciplinary love, and tough love in order to grow into the amazing adults for which they are destined.

For many years I suffered from low self-esteem, feelings of inadequacy, fear of allowing anyone to get close to me and poor choices driven by the need for the type of love I somehow missed in my span of growth and development. I made decisions without seeking wise counsel because I felt alone in the world.

But I knew that I was different. I did not understand why I had to endure all the things that happened along the journey. Why was I the one who always got hurt and used by people when all I desired was to love and be loved? I had a baby out of wedlock in my twenties which at the time I thought was a mistake that would derail my life forever, only to have that very baby save my life. Because you see, there came a dark time in my life when I thought death surely had to be better. I could not bring myself to leave that baby on this earth without a mother.

The baby is the very thing that changes the trajectory of my life, giving me the love that I needed to receive and to give. That small, crying, needy bundle of pure love gave me the beginning journey to genuine, true, warm and powerful love. I am so thankful for her today. Because of her I am a better person, but it did not happen right away. Buckle up as we talk about it.

At 17, I met this wonderful guy, and we became a couple even though I was too young to truly understand the truth in that word. He was older than I which I thought was amazing in and of itself. What could he possibly see in me and he was a grown man?

Anyway, we were together a few years before the baby came along and he was a good man. He tried to take care of me, and he was a great provider. My young age proved to be problematic as well as my views on love, but our relationship survived and did well until I turned 24. He was a great father and did a fabulous job with our baby, but there was so much missing in the relationship because it was missing in me. I did not know anything about communication. I was selfish in so many ways, but he managed to still do his best for me.

Because I was incomplete, young, unsure, and sad inside it became hard for me to believe that he genuinely loved me and was not trying to control as others had in my past. My inability to communicate my needs effectively and the self-doubt that he really did love me eventually led to the demise of our relationship. I proceeded to destroy the relationship with the first person that attempted to show me unconditional love. It has taken me many years, many mistakes to realize the truth of my life but I realize that every situation, GOD meant it for my good.

I became a single mother and at times I   struggled to make ends meet. But the same man that tried to love me beyond my past helped me cement the future I needed by helping me graduate with a degree in Nursing. I am eternally grateful that despite how I may have treated him he helped me become the woman I am today. Now do not think this happened overnight. This same man hurt by my choices set out to try to destroy me out of his pain. He sued me for custody and attempted to take that beautiful baby away from me. We had some terrible fights, but can I say GOD is a repairer of the breach. Even when we are too dumb to make a decent decision, HE still reigns and will bring all things full circle. I owe all to GOD because HE is the true way to change.

My baby has grown up to be a phenomenal woman, and I am so proud to be called her mother. The great man that is her father and her daddy has become a dear friend that I now honor. We have been able to overcome multiple obstacles that for years did not allow us to be friends through and by the grace of GOD.

GOD'S grace kept us all to be able to see better days, mend broken relationships and recognize that I can do all things through CHRIST who is my strength. I want every woman to know that even at the darkest times in your life that joy truly does come in the morning. Your mistakes may slow you down, but they do not have to derail your life.

When the waves of life toss you around, and it seems they are going to overtake you, remember that it can only last 24 hours, and a new day will begin. A brand-new opportunity to start again. Too often when we make a mistake, we are quick to throw in the towel instead of just starting fresh the next day.

You can make it with the help of GOD, a good therapist, and family/friends. I know because I was once in the dark place that threatened to overtake me, but I woke up the next day to new mercies.

Thank You so much for allowing me to share one of the roads on which I have journeyed. There is more to come so stay tuned!

# CHAPTER 5

For we wrestle not against flesh and blood, but against principalities, against powers, against the rulers of the darkness of this world, against wickedness in high places.

**Ephesians 6:12 (King James Version)**

**Blessed Quietness**
**By: Minister Diane Pace**

Blessed quietness! Holy quietness! What assurance in my soul! I am a living testimony that God will give you perfect peace. God gives a peace that no man can understand (Philippians 4:7) and the peace of God, which surpasses all understanding, will guard your hearts and minds through Christ Jesus. When we walk in spiritual authority, we can humble ourselves. The unction of the Holy Spirit will let us know when to speak and when to be silent. There have been many times along this Christian journey that I could have spoken bitterness. I could have cussed someone out or even ripped their emotions to shreds with my mouth. There were times that I wanted to say some harsh words to some awful people. There were times that my garments and outward appearance were frowned upon. I've experienced people that say they are sanctified Christians yet they're jealous of the anointing that's on my life. The same sanctified Christians get upset every time God opens a door for me. But the God in me always smiles and says, "Bless you my brother or bless you, my sister. There were many times along this journey that I was down for the count. But glory to God I was able to bounce back from life's blows.

Thank God for guarding my mouth and bridling my tongue. (Psalm 141:3) Set a guard, O Lord, before my mouth; keep the door of my lips. I thank God for blessing me to know when to speak. God blessed me to keep my mouth closed and continue studying the word. God is not concerned with our outward appearance but the matters of the heart. (1 Peter 3:3-4) Whose adorning let it not be that outward adorning of plaiting the hair, and of wearing of gold, or of putting on of apparel; But let it be the hidden man of the heart, in that which is not corruptible, even the ornament of a meek and quiet spirit, which is in the sight of God of great price. God does not look at the outward appearance. The hair, the jewelry, and the clothes mean nothing. God looks at the inner man. God is searching for a meek and quiet spirit. His word says, "A quiet spirit is more valuable to him." When someone is talking foolish or saying hurtful things just to get a response, I look at that devil with the authority which God has given me and say, "To God Be the Glory" or "Blessed Assurance Jesus Is Mine." I must know who I am. I'm a child of the King! And I'm walking in spiritual authority. I shut up and allow God to do the speaking. I thank God for blessing me to know when to speak. (Ecclesiastes 3:7) A time to rend, and a time to sew; a time to keep silence, and a time to speak; When I get ready to speak on something that I know is not pleasing to God I shut up and began to pray. (Psalm 19:14) Lord please, "Let the words of my mouth, and the meditation of my heart, be acceptable in thy sight, O LORD, my strength, and my redeemer." In other words, let my mouth speak nothing but what is true, kind, and profitable. My heart meditates nothing but what is holy and pure. I choose to walk worthy of calling myself a Christian. The only way I can walk worthy is to surrender all of me to God. Surrendering all means I must yield to the power of God. I must love people regardless of how they carry themselves. I am a child of God, and I have chosen to walk worthy.

After I launched my first book as a published author Walking Worthy was birthed. Walking Worthy is my outreach ministry. The scripture God gave me for my outreach ministry is Colossians 1:10. That ye may walk worthy of the Lord unto all pleasing, being fruitful in every good work, and increasing in the knowledge of God. Some people chose not to support my book simply because they played no part in it. What those naysayers did not know, was that it was a prophecy.

On May 28, 2017, during the altar call it was prophesied that I would write books. In early 2018, I met my Publisher Felicia Lucas at a Polish Your Diamond seminar. Felicia explained to me that she was looking for authors to be a part of her Anthology. At that moment, the prophecy never crossed my mind. In fact, it wasn't until after the book launched and I began to see that the naysayers had chosen not to support the book. Some thought their dirty laundry was being aired and some just simply had their reasons. Keep in mind these were people that call themselves sanctified Christians. My husband and I were so disappointed by the negative behavior of people that say they are "saved." Yet, we kept our mouths closed and took it to God in prayer. (Proverbs 17:27-28) He who has knowledge spares his words, and a man of understanding is of a calm spirit. Even a fool is counted wise when he holds his peace; when he shuts his lips, he is considered perceptive.

I had gotten to the point that I was asking God what makes mankind so jealous. When we say we are Christians, doesn't that mean to be Christ-like? Where is it written that Christ was like this? Why can't those of us that claim to be Christians be happy and supportive of others? I could remember being in the presence of some Christians and I felt like Superman around kryptonite. God reminded me that every one that is saved is not delivered.

Ephesians 6:12 For we wrestle not against flesh and blood, but against principalities, against powers, against the rulers of the darkness of this world, against wickedness in high places. Isaiah 58:3 tells us that sin separates us from God. My mind went back to when I first answered my calling into ministry. I was told that everyone can't go where I'm going. I must say, after Down for The Count launched, I had to deal with some serious demons. Again, these were people that call themselves sanctified Christians. I remember spending so much time praying seeking Godly wisdom.

Two weeks later, God began to let me know these are doors that He had opened for me. As I was praying one day, God spoke to my spirit and said, "This is the prophecy that Prophetess Julia Walker had spoken to you last year," "It was my promise that you would write books." God let me know that I didn't need to apologize to anyone for being blessed. I didn't need to apologize because I'm anointed. I didn't need to apologize because he was exalting me. Glory to God! I was able to bounce back from life's blows. God is my keeper. Psalm 121:5 The LORD is thy keeper: the LORD is thy shade upon thy right hand. God guards my mouth. Proverbs 21:23, Whoso keepeth his mouth and his tongue keepeth his soul from troubles.

(Isaiah 30:15) "For thus saith the Lord GOD, the Holy One of Israel; In returning and rest shall ye be saved; in quietness and in confidence shall be your strength: and ye would not." We must be born again, and when we are born again Christians turning to God, He will give us rest. I had to trust in God, full of calmness and of peace. All praise belongs to God; none of the foolishness made me bitter it made me better. It didn't break me; it made me stronger. I was down for the count, but by the grace of God, I remained steadfast and immovable always abounding in the works of the Lord. I know that my labor in the Lord is not in vain. Amen. (Romans 15:13) "May the God of hope fill you with all joy and peace as you trust in him, so that you may overflow with hope by the power of the Holy Spirit."

# CHAPTER 6

"Call unto me, and I will answer thee, and shew thee great and mighty things, which thou knowest not."

## Jeremiah 33: 3 (King James Version)

**A Walk of Faith**
**By: Nanyamka A. Payne**

## Faith and Dedication

Thank God church is almost over, and I can't wait to order my favorite 5 wings with fried rice; hold the onions and scallions from the carryout.

This humorous thought often runs through my mind as I sit and listen to the preacher and find it hard to function past my belly when I'm hungry. It sounds like a thunderstorm peeking through the clouds waiting to pour down havoc.

As the hunger pains increase so does my wiggling, talking and squirming but still not paying attention to what is being said. The revival is going great! And all I kept dreaming about was those wings hitting the roof of my mouth and him saying finally saying "Amen."

1. Have you ever experienced such intense withdrawals when you're hungry?
2. How did you handle it?

The body works in both mysterious and peculiar ways, and the mind controls it all.

Can you imagine what my face was looking like?

- What does your face look like when you're hungry? **Have fun! Draw it in the open space.**

As the preacher closes out his sermon, something hits me in my gut. POW!

The overwhelming sensation I feel is not from food but the guilt and shame of not living a more dedicated life to serving God. I grew up in the church and still there as my father is my Pastor of 14 years but should be further along in my faith walk.

To recognize this problem was both a blessing and a curse in disguise. To go through the motions, faking it and pretending to be living right was a recipe for the sickness that pushed its way right next to that hunger I was feeling.

I asked myself "Why am I at this moment in all of my 36 years of living?"

In life, you will experience awakening moments of both purpose and defining who you are. In this, I realized I was taking up God-given space for granted and needed to focus on what I was called to do in this life. My purpose was rebirthed. I gained back my focus and assured myself that I would be my best from this day forward.

1. Have you found your purpose?
2. Do you know what it is?
3. And are you living it out?

As the Preacher said "Amen," I quickly made a B line to the altar to make some tough decisions but needed faith to do it. I spoke with the preacher and his wife, and through prayer, I dedicated my life back to God. It was not an easy choice, but it was what I needed so that I could share this triumph with you.

1. How did I do it?

**Tips:** Through counseling, fasting, prayer and cleaning up bad habits that did not yield results of growth.

Through faith, I learned that dedication is a full-time, worth and risk it all forever commitment.

## **Faith and Through Losing it ALL**

"Welcome to the company, and we are pleased to meet you." What a very pretty smile I often heard as I was the face and voice of this national Dining Brand for the next 7 years.

I take pride in serving from excellence, but as time went on, I felt myself losing faith to stay at a demanding job. The smile faded the last 3 years; my patience had worn thin like the edges of my hair and being hospitalized was the straw that broke the camel's back.

I would exam my paycheck as if the numbers would magically change overnight, but equal compensation was not being met for the job I was doing. I remained steadfast and unmoved due to not wanting to start over on another job, face being homeless, lose my car or file unemployment.

I loved eating, so a perk of employment was free meals, so I ignored the lack of respect I was given and unfair wages.

1. Have you ever stayed at a job where the "other" contributing factors outweighed what you deserved?

If you answered "yes," this description of Faith and Through Losing It All will help wholly heal and restore you.

I aggressively applied for jobs, went on interviews but NOTHING was coming through! And on top of my searching my car was repossessed because I could not keep up with the payments.

1. Are you currently looking for another job while working and why?

I am at my desk and happy to know I will be getting off in 27 minutes and getting dinner. I glance down for a split second, and both the director and my manager are at the desk. I rush to close my notepad as I did not want my "To Do" list showing. **1) Leave my job in the next 30 days! Boy, did God work quickly!** "Nan, may we speak with you?" "Sure." As I sit in the meeting the only words I hear, "I'm sorry, but we are going to have to let you go." I kindly thanked them for the notice and never looked back.

I lost my car, money, friends, my job but never faith. I was unemployed for 3 months until I finally got that email I was praying for. "We are pleased to offer." As tears of joy poured from my eyes and the taste of salt pierced my lips, I knew it was all worth this journey.

1. How did I make it through?

**Tips:**

- I let it ALL go without fear, hesitation, worrying, stressing or questioning this process.

Through faith, I learned that I had to lose it all before I gained everything I needed!

## Faith and Grief: 1 Thessalonians 4:13 – 18

"Oh, no! Is there anything I can do? I am on my way."

I will never forget the sound of those 2 words for the rest of my life!

I overheard my father yell out one recent Saturday morning at 6:23 as the walls in the living room rushed into focus, I stood still, and the tears began to pour from my eyes. I muster up enough strength to get up again, stand, fall down but remain seated this time until my father appears from the upstairs at my parents' home to give me the untimely news.

As I lie back now in a fetal position, a heat wave causes my temperature to rise from head to toe followed up by an excruciating headache as I think about what I just heard.

Have you ever felt a sudden cascade of temperatures in your body that left you feeling this way?

If your answer was "yes," this description of faith and grief will resonate loudly with you.

The impact of his words felt like a crash!

My heart and brain instantly felt alone.

Do not be afraid of death; we will all die one day.

The shock of death doesn't come easy, it stings and hurts like crazy not knowing when it will happen but keep preparing as best as you know how until it comes.

1. Have you prepared for this day?
2. And are you ready to meet God?

As I processed this recent news, I immediately start recalling all the things I will no longer be afforded to since his passing. I know it "just" happened, but it felt like I was in a bad dream and could not wake-up fast enough.

- No more birthday phone calls.
- No more text messages "I'm rooting for you, I'm proud of you, Merry Christmas."

- No more mentor tips or counseling sessions about life, business, finance, and relationships.

As I searched for answers, I needed a place of peace, quiet and comfort to process knowing that I will never see my great friend of 20 plus years again.

1. How did I find it?

**Tips:**

- Remembering the fun times and reminiscing on how awesome it was to experience friendship.
- Prayer, counseling, spending time with family, friends and cherishing life more.
- The comfort of knowing he was a saved man in heaven, and I'll see him again soon.

Through faith, I learned how to cope with death in a more positive manner and take each day as it comes.

In the spaces below, write down 3 dates in <u>your</u> life that changed <u>your</u> view on Faith and the lessons learned.

**Date #1:**_____

**What happened?**

_____

_____

_____

_____

**Lesson learned:**

_____

_____

_____

_____

**Date #2:** _____

**What happened?**

_____

_____

_____

_____

**Lesson learned:**

_____

_____

_____

_____

**Date #3:** _____

**What happened?**

_____

_____

_____

_____

**Lesson learned:**

_____

_____

_____

_____

**Thoughts to Think About:** After embracing the uncertainty of outcomes, you can now walk boldly forward knowing that this process was to grow, strengthen, nurture, mature and humble you for your

NEXT. <u>Do not</u> be afraid to remember where <u>you</u> came from, what <u>you</u> learned and how it taught <u>you</u> that faith is truly an act of God.

**Verse:** 2 Corinthians 5:7 **(KJV)**

**Questions:** Check your heart space

1. Do <u>you</u> know him?
2. Do <u>you</u> trust him?

# CHAPTER 7

Let the message of Christ dwell among you richly as you teach and admonish one another with all wisdom through psalms, hymns, and songs from the Spirit, singing to God with gratitude in your hearts.

**Colossians 3:16 (New International Version)**

## Leaving the Church to Becoming the Church
## By: Louvanta White

Before I pen this chapter. I would like to take this moment to thank every gem who is reading this chapter. I'm not out to defame or bring shame to anyone's name or Character. I am here as a woman of God to help build up the kingdom so our people can stop perishing from lack of knowledge. Without further due, let's explore how I took church hurt and turned it around to be the example of how we, the church is supposed to treat one another.

Have you ever known you were called or chosen to do something? Have you ever found yourself resisting or running from your gifts? I have a better question. Have you ever downplayed your spiritual gifts or anointing because you didn't want to offend anybody? Well, I too can definitely relate to all these questions.

When I was younger, I always knew I was different. When I was younger, I was often told by family, teachers, and even strangers " You are different" God has a plan for you. I'm not even going to lie to you all because I wasn't trying to hear that. I was ok doing me. Although I knew about God, I still ignored the signs of submitting to him. When it came to religion and church, I really didn't know what it meant. All I knew was we had to go on Sundays. But that still didn't move me to want to be around church folks. Like many, I used to say the famous saying. "I'M GOOD." "GOD KNOWS MY HEART."

Bear with me you guys. As I'm penning this, the tears are falling. Ok, where was I? When I gave my life to Christ, I was 16. As a teenager I had friends who ministered to me. They were active at church, but I still was reluctant to dig deeper about learning what church meant. Actually, my ex-boyfriend was the one who had me coming to church. You see this church was the first church I joined. I was a part of the youth activities, choir, summer camp, etc. The youth, we were like family. When we were going through our own challenges, we all felt it. As we all were getting older, we started to prep for college and live our lives. We also started to see the contradictions and hypocrisy which led me to leave. I was hurt because the youth looked up to me and I felt I let them down, but I had to go. For years I would just visit different churches. I never joined but just visited. Fast forward to 2009. In 2009 my life was going great. I graduated from college. I was excited. God was up to something. Well, August I found out I was pregnant with my daughter. I was shocked because I was on birth control(laughing). Again God was up to something. When I told you all that my life changed, I meant that.

December 2009 my job forced me to take my maternity leave early, I was hurt and devastated. I didn't know what to do. My thoughts were OMG! How am I going to do this without any money? Sometimes maternity leaves took longer to process, and I still had bills coming in. But God! I cried, and it was that cry that I knew I had to get back right with God. So I remember crying and crying. I got into the submission and surrendering position. I told God if you work this out for me, that I would go to church again.

God showed up for me, and I kept my word to him. I found another church home. Although I was happy and on fire for God. I found myself at a church where it was cliquish. Although the pastor was a good leader, some of the members were just stuck in their ways. I found myself at a place where I was unhappy. My worship turned from authentic praise to just routine church praise. I remember addressing the issues, but it all was downplayed, and I was looked like the bad guy. They played church but didn't want to be the church. So of course, I left. What hurt me the most was I came in with a sincere heart and wanted to serve the people. Once I saw how they treated me, I felt church wasn't real. It took me back to that hurt place when I was 16. I felt like I revisited that same thing over again.

Although that hurt me, I continued my relationship with God. I said I wasn't going back to another church. While not serving in a church. I begin to feel like I was missing something. One of my confidants had a long talk with me. She said Cookie, church is like the hospital for the sick. We are trying to get better. She said although you feel like the church let you down, God didn't. She said, and besides, you are not at church for them. You are there to deepen your relationship with God and to bring souls to God. She gave me a lot of knowledge and wisdom, but those key points helped me change my viewpoint on churches. God saw fit for me to join Trinity United Church of Christ. Currently, I'm still there. I'm being fed spiritually, emotionally, mentally, and physically.

When it comes to church hurt, I learned how to extend grace and mercy towards those who may display ungodly characteristics. I thank God for not giving up on me and for allowing that pain to help me with my purpose. Today I can show love even if it's not returned. I am forever grateful to serve in the building church as well as being the church.

## How to Deal with Church Hurt

1. Pray, Pray, and pray. Praying helps us to hear God's voice. It also helps us enter the healing process. We must keep in mind that the church sometimes doesn't always imitate Christ. That's why it is important for us to lead by example and help build the kingdom. It's also important to teach and display the characteristics of Jesus in front of others. All may not adhere, but you will reach someone.

2. Address the church member or members. We know the saying goes everything doesn't need a

response, but sometimes you must address things especially when they out of order.

3. Forgive I know this is hard to do but in order for us to have peace and a healthy spiritual life, we have to forgive. God forgives us even when we don't deserve it.

4. Separate mankind from the church. Not everyone in church is bad people or have bad intentions. There are still some good people out there.

5. Don't render hurt for hurt. Don't seek revenge or make others pay for your past church hurts. That isn't fair to others or right to do. When you are in church, let the spirit lead you to the right ministry for you and the people whom you need to minister to.

6. Be the example. Continue to let your light shine. Continue to display Christ-like characteristics.

I can admit church hurt doesn't feel good on many levels. The pain you feel will have you acting rebellious and even turning against God. When you accept your spiritual calling, and you serve in church. Keep in mind sanctification is a lifelong process. Church, it's time for us to represent Jesus and bring souls back to God. Playing church is over. It's time to come together and be the church. I hope this chapter was a blessing to you all. Thanks, Ms. Beautiful Gem.

# CHAPTER 8

Be strong and courageous.  Do not be afraid, do not be discouraged, for the Lord your God will be with you wherever you go.

**Joshua 1:9 (New International Version)**

**Returning to the Scene of the Crime**
**By:  Minister Felicia C. Lucas**

For over twenty years, I have worked as a Retail Manager and more specifically as a General Manager for the past nine years.  Since my first retail job as a part-time cashier in high school and college, I have enjoyed working in this industry.  For the most part, the overall experience has been rather pleasant.  On December 13, 2018, my life changed forever.

I had just worked a 2pm to midnight shift at my store. I had come home and began to settle down for the night. I decided to pop in a movie while I began to doze off. I was happy about being off the next workday since I had put in a lot of hours during the earlier part of the week. I had been in bed for about an hour, and my cell phone rang. I looked at the caller ID, and it was my boss calling. I looked at my phone and said, "He must have called me by mistake. He wouldn't be calling me this time of night." I didn't answer his call initially. Immediately, he called back, and I then knew it was not a mistake. He proceeded to inform me that my store had just been robbed.

I was in total shock! I was just there! My heart started beating rapidly, and then his next statement shook me to the core! He stated that my assistant manager had been kidnapped from her home during a home invasion and was forced to go to the store. OH MY GOD!!! At that point, he provided me the gruesome details of the whole ordeal.

I got dressed and drove to my store to meet my boss, the police and crime scene investigators. As I was driving to the store, many thoughts begin to enter my head.

- That could have been me

- I wonder if the robbers had planned to rob the store when we were there
- Do they know where I live too?
- Is my assistant manager going to be ok?
- Who could have done this?
- Why did they do this?

I also experienced a mixed bag of emotions that overtook me all at once:

- Fear-Scared it could happen again
- Anger-Why did the robbers violate my store and my assistant's home?
- Gratitude-Thankful that I did not experience it firsthand

As I returned to the scene of the crime, I knew I had been affected by this extremely traumatic event. My biggest job at this point was to be a rock to my employees as we dealt with the aftermath of such a horrific event. I had to personally share with my staff the events that occurred, and some were shaken up about what happened. I knew some of my leadership team was silently dealing with the situation and I suggested to them to seek professional counseling services. I took my own advice and connected with a therapist who has helped me during this traumatic experience.

As a result of this experience, I was affected in many areas of my life.

- Physically: For some time after this event, I had bags under my eyes, was extremely tired, extreme headaches and very little sleep. My heart was constantly beating rapidly, and every time I went to the scene of the crime, I was physically sick.
- Mentally: As my mind kept racing day after day, I played the thoughts over and over in my mind, The What Ifs!
- Emotionally: I was crying at the drop of a hat. I was trying to be strong for my staff at work but at home and would break down and cry. As I faced the area that the crime occurred, day after day, it took time for me to be strong enough to enter the building without breaking down.
- Spiritually: I could not even pray for myself. I wanted to talk to God, but I could not say anything. I had to turn to my worship music as a way to cope. I am so thankful for my spiritual mentor and my husband who were praying for me. I shared with some of the prayer warriors about what had happened to me.

- REAL TALK: During this time of vulnerability, those whom I thought would be there for me or at least check on me, did not even reach back out. So not only was I dealing with the trauma, I quickly recognized who was really in my corner.

- Professionally: This incident had me questioning some things about my career. Was I in the right place? Was it time for me to do something else? My spiritual mentor shared with me that God was not going to immediately move me from the pain. He was going to heal me during the pain so I can be ready for my next! Wow! God was going to show me how much he really loved me and cared for me even though I was experiencing one of my biggest blows in life. He was going to help me to get through this situation!

I have four tips that have enabled me to function daily as I returned to my job each day. Has the experience changed me? Absolutely! I have learned so much about my strength and how others are able to overcome the very hard places in life. This experience has drawn me closer to God, and I know even more so that He loves me!

Tip #1: Get therapy to help work through traumatic situations- There is a stigma concerning mental health in the church and more, especially the African American community. The Bible says in 3 John 1:2, Beloved, I wish above all things that thou mayest prosper and be in health, even as thy soul prospereth. God is not just talking about our physical health, but he also desires that we are healthy mentally.

Tip #2: Acknowledge the incident occurred- It is certainly fine to talk about what happened. It was necessary for me to communicate regularly with my assistant manager and my staff. Talking about it helped us all heal, and it strengthened us to keep moving. When we are silent as a result of a trauma, it can slow down our actual healing process.

Tip # 3: Engage in normal activities as much as possible-I chose to not retreat at home and not to be afraid to return to work. That was a process though, I must admit. Initially, I was observing every strange car in my neighborhood and any person who looked suspect as they walked into the store. I had to decide to not allow the trauma to keep me stuck. I am so sure that if my relationship with God had not been at a good place, I would not have been able to get back up again to move forward to my greater purpose.

Tip #4: Find your stress reduction zone- I gravitated towards exercise, worship music, and essential oils to help reduce my stress versus turning to food as I have done in the past to cope with extreme stress. Instead of me gaining weight during this experience, I have lost twenty-five pounds since the incident. I am still moving towards my best me yet!

In conclusion, traumatic experiences can literally knock a person to their lowest points in life. The key is what do you do to get back up again. With God and my support system (husband, therapist and spiritual mentor) I was able to bounce back and move forward. I have come so far these past few months, and I am thankful that God has healed some and is still healing some of my wounds.

# About the Co-Authors

## VISIONARY AUTHOR, FELICIA C. LUCAS

Felicia Lucas is a #1 International Best-Selling Author and 4 Time Best Selling Author, Speaker, Coach and Book Publisher. Minister Felicia and her husband, Pastor Kelvin Lucas, co-founded *Take It By Force Ministries*, Inc. a non-profit youth and young adult 501©3 organization and *Dominion Tabernacle Church*. They were married in 1997 and have three children.

As a business woman on the move, she is the CEO of *His Glory Creations Publishing, LLC* and the Co-Founder of *His Glory Creations Christian Store*, an online Christian and Inspirational Store.

She is the 2016 Recipient of the North Carolina Career Woman of the Year Award by the North Carolina Business and Professional Women's Club.

Felicia graduated from the University of North Carolina at Chapel Hill with a Bachelor of Arts Degree in Speech Communication. For over twenty years, she has worked in the human resources field.

www.felicialucas.com

www.hisglorycreations.com

www.takeitbyforce.net

Facebook: Author and Speaker Felicia Lucas

Facebook: His Glory Creations Publishing LLC

Facebook: Take it by Force Ministries, Inc.

Instagram: Coach Felicia Lucas

Twitter: Movetoyourbestu

## **Other literary works by Felicia Lucas:**

- Make it Happen: Moving Towards Your Best U!
- Get in the Game: A Teen's Playbook for Winning the Game of Life
- The Bounce Back: Triumphant Stories of Resiliency and Perseverance
- Down for the Count: Bouncing Back from Life's Blows-Volume I
- Stuff: A Collection of Middle Schools Thoughts

## AUTHOR DR. PATRICE CAGLE

Dr. Patrice Cagle resides in North Carolina. She is a Postdoctoral Research Associate conducting cancer research and is the author of "*My Sustainer.*" Dr. Cagle loves animals, as well as reading, relaxing, and spending time with her family. During her spare time, she enjoys giving back to her community where she has volunteered for animal groups and organizations combating abuse and domestic violence.

She is very involved in her church, Monument of Faith Ministries in Eden, NC, where she teaches children's church, sings in multiple choirs, and is an adviser for the Youth Choir. She currently is a member of several scientific professional societies and has been an ambassador for the local American Cancer Society chapter. Dr. Cagle has also been the guest speaker for cancer-related and domestic violence events.

Email: mysustainerpc@yahoo.com
Website: www.mysustainerpc.com
Facebook, Instagram, and Twitter: @mysustainer

## AUTHOR MARY HOOKS

Mary Hooks grew up in Milwaukee, Wisconsin where the street life tried to take her out. She was a teen mom involved in prostitution, drug/alcoholism, and domestic violence. What the enemy meant for evil, God turned for good.

Today, Mary's mission is to help young women that are battling with the same issues she has overcome, as well as prevent others from falling into such a dark lifestyle.

She is a speaker, author, and influencer. Saved by God's grace. Through her testimony, Mary inspires, encourages, and motivates others. She is the author of *"Be Completely Comfortable with the Unique Way God Made You"*.

Email: hooksmary49@gmail.com
Instagram: maryhooks18

## AUTHOR PAMELA HORNE

Elder Pamela Horne was born the fourth child of eight in Island County, Washington State. She was raised and educated in Durham, NC. A woman of God with a compassion for ministering to broken women, she has a heart for seeing men and women delivered, restored and renewed in Christ.

In 1988, she earned a Bachelor's degree from Western Carolina University in Radio/TV and Journalism, a Bachelor's degree in Christian Education and Biblical Studies in 2011 from the Durham Extension of the United Christian College of Goldsboro, NC.

Elder Horne began her ministry under Pastor Dr. Mae V. Horne of Gateway to Heaven UHCA. She was ordained under Chief Apostle William D. Lee in 2012. In 2015, her vision for Consuming Fire Ministries was birthed. She continues her ministry work at Gateway to Heaven UHC. She recently retired from the Durham County Sheriff's Office (Detention Division) after over 27 years of service. Currently, she serves as the Co-Director and Event Planner of The Women of Triumph Ministries. She is a true worshipper and loves music & singing.

Facebook: Consuming Fire Book Ministries

Email: consumingfirebooks@gmail.com

## AUTHOR JOCELIN T. HOOD MCELDERRY

A new author with intentions to pen several more best-selling books sharing her life and career journey. Recently retired from Wake County, she has been an RN for 33 years and is now jumping into the world of entrepreneurship. She has multiple projects she is currently working on and is excited about the journey.

She receives a great deal of joy from serving others and sharing her life's passions. She is an avid reader as well as a lifelong learner.

She is a GOD chaser and loves GOD with all her being as she serves in her church, The Well Church in

Raleigh, NC. She has one child, Nicollette, and one grandson, Cameron. She is a lifelong resident of Clayton, NC.

Email: Jocelintmcelderry@gmail.com

Facebook: Jocelin T. Hood

Instagram: @jocelintmcelderry

Twitter: @jocelintmcelderry

## AUTHOR DIANE PACE

Minister Diane Pace was born in Smithfield, NC and now resides in Wendell, NC. Diane is the daughter of the late Willie Harvey Turner II and Frances Turner. Through that union, she is the youngest of seven siblings.

She is a loving wife to her husband, Raymond Pace. She is a mother of six children, nine grandchildren and one great-grandchild.

Diane is the founder of the organization, Walking Worthy. In 2018, she was also a co-author in Down for The Count, Volume One: Bouncing Back from Life's Blows.

She is a member of Women of Triumph Ministries and serves as a minister at Delightful Temple Ministries in Kenly, NC under the leadership of Pastor Carolynn Robinson. In 2019, Diane received her Associates Degree in

Biblical Studies from Safe Haven Interdenominational Bible College and Training Institute.

Email: walkingworthyisa@yahoo.com

https://walkingworthyisa.wixsite.com/mysite

## AUTHOR NANYAMKA PAYNE

Nanyamka Payne is the 4th child of 7 born to Pastor Ricardo and Mary Payne. She was born and raised in the Washington, DC area.

By day she is an Administrative Assistant for the Government. In her free time, she enjoys traveling, bowling, spending time with her family and entering contests and has won over 200 and counting. By faith, she knows the ultimate prize is showing up for the opportunity!

She has been speaking to her congregation every Sunday morning for the last 3 years through her ministry called *Winners University* and affectionately calls them "Winners!" After sharing her faith lesson of the week, she randomly blesses a member with a gift and to include visitors.

She thanks God for his continued trust in her and child-like faith.

Facebook: Nanyamka Payne

Facebook: *Winners* University

Instagram: IAmNanyamka

Pinterest: IAmNanyamka

Twitter: IAmNanyamka

Hashtags: #intensifiedwinner

Email: iamnanyamka@gmail.com

## AUTHOR LOUVANTA WHITE

Louvanta White-Horne, also known as "Cookie," is an inspirational and motivational speaker, spiritual life coach, and Author.

She is the founder of Refining Stepping Stones Into Beautiful Gems outreach ministry. Her ministry is designed to help women bring back their self-love, not being ashamed of who they are, and embracing who they are called to be. Louvanta is very passionate about deepening her relationship with God and ministering to others.

She is a proud mother of her beautiful daughter Katrina and enjoys being in love with the love of her life. Louvanta enjoys spending time with her family and close friends, reading, eating, dancing, shopping, and most importantly chasing after God's heart.

Facebook: Louvanta Horne

Email:beautifulgem84@yahoo.com

## Notes

## Notes

## Notes

# Notes

## Notes